BOOK TITLE:

WHAT DO YOU

DO AFTER YOU

HAVE PRAYED?

ERIC JOSEPH

COPYRIGHT PAGE

COPYRIGHT © 2024 BY ERIC W. JOSEPH. ALL RIGHTS RESERVED.

Book paperback edition: January 2024

Book design, Cover design, and eBook design by:

Shefa R.@srumby17
Publisher: Amazon KDP

TABLE OF CONTENT

INTRODUCTION

In the fabric of our faith, prayer is the lifeline that connects us to God, a lifeline that comes through our Lord and Savior, Jesus Christ. Welcome to the voyage of discovery and transformation found inside the pages of "What Do You Do After You Have Prayed." This book is more than simply a list of words; it is an investigation, a handbook, and a friend for those who have prayed sincerely and are looking for guidance and answers.

Every Christian may have been asked, "What do you do after you have prayed?" It speaks to the need for hope, meaning, and a real relationship with God amid the chaos of everyday life. This book aims to offer meaningful responses through biblical stories, practical insights, and a wealth of Christian wisdom.

We will explore critical tenets of the Christian faith in the upcoming chapters, including the transformational potential of prayer and the processes of asking for direction, exercising wisdom, and seeing divine involvement. Every chapter reads like a trip, telling the tales of people who, like us, have faced difficulties, had to make choices, and found comfort in following God's lead.

We will critically examine the ideas of active waiting, the relationship between faith and action, and the value of getting advice from those on the same spiritual path. With scriptural references, real-world examples, and helpful advice, my goal is to arm you with the means to react successfully to God's intervention in your life.

Open your heart to the possibilities beyond every prayer as you embark on this adventure. Allow this book to be a source of motivation, direction, and personal growth as you confidently and purposefully negotiate life's many twists and turns. I pray that it will act as a lighthouse, showing you the path to a life surrounded by God's guidance and unwavering presence.

CHAPTER 1: THE LIFE-CHANGING POWER OF PRAYER

For Christians, prayer is the lifeblood of their connection with God, not just a ritual. This chapter sets out to investigate the enormous impact that prayer may have on our lives, taking its cue from the living Word of God. We learn how a consistent, sincere connection with God may strengthen our faith by looking at biblical instances of prayers being answered. As we are reminded in Psalm 145:18 (NIV), "The Lord is near to all who call on him, to all who call on him in truth." Prayer is a conduit between us and the Divine, allowing us to express our most private hopes, anxieties, and thanks.

Stories of prayers answered abound throughout the Bible, showing that God hears, sees, and acts. Hannah's account in 1 Samuel 1:27 (NIV), whose sincere request for a child was granted, is one such instance. Her steadfast faith shows us the value of praying consistently. In Matthew 7:7 (NIV), Jesus tells us that our heavenly Father hears and answers our sincere requests, so we should ask, seek, and knock.

This highlights the significance of having a regular and intense prayer life in times of crisis and regular dialogue with God. Prayer is not just a way to ask for blessings; it's also a way to demonstrate thankfulness, as Philippians 4:6-7 (NIV) tells us to "not be anxious about anything, but in every situation, by prayer and petition, with thanksgiving, present your requests to God."

Although life's obstacles might be difficult, prayer gives us the courage to face them head-on. Psalm 34:17-18 (NIV) reminds us, "The righteous cry out, and the Lord hears them; he delivers them from all their troubles. The Lord is close to the brokenhearted and saves those crushed in spirit."

Prayer acts as a compass to help us navigate the ups and downs of our lifelong spiritual journey. By embracing the transforming power of prayer, we promote change, growth, and a deeper relationship with God. As noted in 1 Thessalonians 5:17 (NIV), which urges us to "pray continually," prayer is not a fast cure but rather a consistent practice that fosters our connection with the Divine. We are joining a fascinating story found in the Bible, one in which God interacts with us daily.

This chapter offers an invitation to unlock the limitless potential that prayer contains for our lives and a journey of spiritual renewal and personal development. Matthew 21:22 (NIV) reiterates the promise that "If you believe, you will receive whatever you ask for in prayer."

CHAPTER 2: SEEK DIRECTION FROM GOD

Determining God's will is one of the most critical and challenging threads to weave into the fabric of our lives. This chapter explores the practice of seeking heavenly guidance by utilizing the Bible's live text as a beacon of light. It looks at how prayer may guide us while making important decisions about our relationships, jobs, and other life events. It is obvious how important it is to ask God for direction as we face life's obstacles.

The lives of biblical figures offer compelling examples of those who sought and followed God's guidance. The Bible provides profound wisdom on this matter, and in Proverbs 3:5–6 (NIV), we are reminded to "Trust in the Lord with all your heart and lean not on your understanding; in all your ways submit to him, and he will make your paths straight." Genesis 12:1-4 (NIV), which describes Abraham's trip, is a powerful story of trust and obedience demonstrating divine guidance's transformational potential.

The narrative of Joseph, found in Genesis 37–50 (NIV), is another inspiring tale of a person who persevered in adhering to God's plan in the face of hardship. His life serves as an example of how wise it is to rely on God's all-powerful direction.

The decisions we make in the area of our jobs have a significant influence on how our lives turn out. We must pray and meditate on God for guidance while considering our career possibilities. We may put our faith in divine wisdom to guide us in making professional decisions, much as David did when faced with difficulties and prayed to God for guidance. The Bible contains timeless truths about relationships. The book of Ruth portrays Ruth's steadfast devotion and dedication to Naomi, highlighting the need to seek God's guidance in our relationships. By praying, we ask God to be a silent accomplice in our relationships, pointing us toward people who share His plan for our lives.

This chapter is an invitation to study the living word, look to the Bible for direction, and include prayer in all the crucial decisions we make. By using biblical knowledge and praying sincerely, we ask God to light our way, ensuring that our choices align with His plan and experiencing the life-changing potential of doing so.

CHAPTER 3: ACTIVELY WAIT

Patience and confidence in God's perfect timing are traits that are not only desirable but crucial at specific points in the complex fabric of our spiritual journey. This chapter takes readers on a deep exploration of the essence of active waiting. It does this by looking at the practical aspects of active waiting and taking great inspiration and wisdom from biblical characters who patiently and trustingly awaited the fulfillment of God's promises.

A foundational text for our comprehension of active waiting is Isaiah 40:31 (ESV). This timeless verse reminds us that when we wait, we can renew our spiritual strength by immersing ourselves in God's promises and putting our complete trust in His perfect timing. "But they who wait for the Lord shall renew their strength; they shall mount up with wings like eagles; they shall run and not be weary; they shall walk and not faint."

An exemplary case of active waiting may be observed in Genesis 15–21 (ESV), which tells the story of Abraham and Sarah. Their experience serves as a tribute to the value of courageous patience. Abraham and Sarah showed that a heart rooted in faith is the key to fulfilling God's promise, even when it seems impossible, by remaining constant despite the unrelenting passage of time and the daunting problems that loomed over them.

Active waiting is a profound art form that is further enhanced by the character of Joseph, mentioned in Genesis 37–50 (ESV). Betrayal and incarceration were interwoven throughout his life story like threads in a tapestry.

Nevertheless, Joseph's ascent and accomplishing God's promises were finally made possible by his unwavering faith in God's divine plan and dedication to righteousness. His narrative shows that God is constructing a great story beyond our comprehension, even during the most challenging waiting seasons. We might use practical tactics as we anxiously anticipate the fulfillment of our petitions, which are at the heart of active waiting.

This scriptural instruction encourages us to take inspiration from the diligent farmer who waits for the precious harvest. James 5:7-8 (ESV) says, "Be patient, therefore, brothers, until the coming of the Lord. See how the farmer waits patiently for the earth's precious fruit until it receives the early and the late rains. You also be patient. Establish your hearts, for the coming of the Lord is at hand." It serves as a reminder that while we wait for God's promises to come to pass, patience should be nurtured.

While practicing the complex skill of active waiting, we may take deliberate Action to advance. We turn times of waiting into chances for spiritual development and becoming ready for God's promises to come to pass by actively attempting to strengthen our faith, lovingly serving others, and continuously praying.

This chapter offers a warm invitation to delve deeper into the critical idea of active waiting. It invites us to explore the depths of the Bible and finds inspiration in the stories of Joseph, Sarah, and Abraham. It inspires us to live the qualities of faith and patience when we impatiently wait for God to answer our prayers.

We may practice active waiting in the same way that these obedient individuals did, knowing that God's promises will be realized in His perfect time.

CHAPTER 4: PUT FAITH INTO ACTION

The Bible demonstrates the dynamic relationship between faith and Action throughout its pages. This chapter examines the idea of faith in Action, using biblical instances and offering real-world applications. It serves as an example of how faith inspires us to take action and apply our values to our day-to-day lives. James 2:17 (ESV) emphasizes the crucial relationship between faith and Action and provides direction. It says, "So also faith by itself if it does not have works, is dead." Our religion is active rather than passive, which drives us to put our convictions into practical acts.

The biblical account of Noah, found in Genesis 6–9 (ESV), eloquently demonstrates faith in Action. God gave Noah the enormous responsibility of building an ark, which demanded steadfast faith and unrelenting Action. Building the ark was a clear example of Noah's faith in Action, showing that faith is more than just a belief—it's a commitment that results in acts that change people's lives.

Think about the doctors and nurses who give their time and expertise freely to give free medical care to underprivileged areas today. Their commitment to serving others is a reflection of the teaching found in Matthew 25:40 (ESV), which states, "And the king will answer them, 'Truly, I say to you, as you did it to one of these, my brothers, you did it to me." Another biblical example is the story of Esther, which is told in the book of Esther (ESV).

Her faith inspired Esther's Action in God, and she risked her life to approach the King and ask for his intervention, ultimately leading to her people's salvation.

In today's world, people who use their position and resources to support social justice issues are examples of faith in Action. They stand for oppressed people, promote equality, and effect positive change. Their actions reflect the biblical call to "seek justice, correct oppression" found in Isaiah 1:17 (ESV). There are many practical ways to live out our faith in the real world, from straightforward acts of kindness like volunteering at a food bank to more involved projects like founding a nonprofit organization to address societal needs. By actively participating in these activities, we reflect the core of our faith and positively impact the world.

With biblical examples and real-world examples, this chapter invites you to investigate the profound relationship between faith and Action. When we embrace faith in Action, we become change agents in our own lives, our communities, and the wider world.

CHAPTER 5:

DIFFERENTIATING BETWEEN FAITH IN ACTION AND ACTIVE WAITING

Two fundamental ideas frequently brought to the core of our faith journey are Active Waiting and Faith in Action. Although these ideas are related, they have important distinctions that any believer should be aware of. Let's examine real-world applications from the Bible and Scripture references to make these distinctions evident.

A great example of active waiting can be found in the lives of Abraham and Sarah, as recorded in Genesis 15–21. They actively waited for the fulfillment of God's promise of a son. Sarah didn't sit idly by; she took matters into her own hands with Hagar. This impatience led to conflict.

Eventually, they learned the value of true Active Waiting, and God blessed them with Isaac. Active Waiting is a patient yet purposeful attitude of expectation. It's like a farmer tending to the soil and watching the seeds he's sown, fully aware that growth takes time.

Take Noah from Genesis 6–9. Noah had faith in God's word, and his faith was manifested in Action as he built the ark. Noah's faith moved him to do something extraordinary, which ultimately led to the preservation of life. On the other hand, Action is when you believe so deeply in God's promises that you take bold steps in alignment with that faith. This is not a passive waiting; it's a dynamic expression of your trust in God.

Active Waiting is clinging to God's promises while letting Him work in His time. An excellent example of this can be found in 1 Samuel 24, where King David, facing imminent death from King Saul, decided to wait it out rather than take matters into his own hands. David's Active Waiting involved putting his faith in God to carry out His promise to establish him as King in His own time and way.

Faith in Action: In 1 Kings 3, David's son Solomon exemplifies the embodiment of faith in Action. Solomon asked for wisdom when God offered him anything, and his faith in God's wisdom enabled him to act wisely as King, making wise decisions, resolving conflicts, and supervising the construction of the magnificent temple in Jerusalem.

Active Waiting: Joseph's story (Genesis 37–50) exemplifies this concept; it entails patiently enduring hardships while having faith in God's plan. Joseph was wrongfully imprisoned but did not waver in his faith; instead, he waited for God's appointed time to emerge as a powerful ruler in Egypt.

Faith in Action: Remember the incredible story of Moses in Exodus 3–4. God called Moses to lead the Israelites out of Egypt, but his fears initially prevented him from accepting the call. Nevertheless, he eventually embraced Faith in Action and led the Israelites through the Red Sea and the wilderness. His faith was active and showed through brave and purposeful deeds.

In conclusion, both concepts are essential to the life of a Christian, and knowing their differences can result in a more fruitful and meaningful journey of faith. Active Waiting emphasizes patient trust in God's timing, often characterized by endurance and reliance on Him. Faith in Action, on the other hand, involves actively living out one's faith, making bold moves and decisions based on trust in God's promises.

CHAPTER 6: OVERCOMING OBSTACLES

Obstacles are the threads that challenge us in the complicated journey of life, but they also offer us the chance to weave perseverance and resilience through faith. This chapter examines overcoming obstacles while taking inspiration from the unwavering determination of biblical heroes who faced and overcame adversity. The Bible is filled with examples of people who showed remarkable determination and endurance in adversity.

One such example is the story of Joseph, which is found in Genesis 37–50. Despite his trials and tribulations, including the betrayal of his brothers and wrongful imprisonment, Joseph clung to his faith in God's plan and emerged as a symbol of triumph over adversity.

The Psalms tell the story of David, a man whose unwavering trust in God's guidance and protection enabled him to overcome seemingly insurmountable challenges, from facing the giant Goliath to navigating the complexities of kingship. These biblical accounts encourage us to cultivate resilience and determination in our own lives so that we can see obstacles as opportunities for growth and refinement rather than as insurmountable barriers and draw strength from God's Word.

Practically speaking, developing resilience and perseverance through faith means appreciating the significance of failures and trials as chances for one's development on both a personal and spiritual level, holding fast to God's plan through hardship, realizing that His purposes go beyond temporary setbacks, and drawing strength from the experiences of the biblical heroes who overcame hardship, realizing that their stories are not merely old tales but live examples of faith's capacity to overcome adversity.

This chapter is an invitation to embrace the transformative power of faith in overcoming obstacles, to view adversity as a catalyst for growth, and to find inspiration from the unwavering spirits of those who walked before us. Through faith, we can rise above life's hurdles, unyielding in our determination to overcome adversity. We can draw from their stories to fuel our resolve and resilience as we face our challenges.

CHAPTER 7: SEEK COUNSELING FROM OTHERS

There are times in the complex framework of our lives when the value of wise counsel from others should be addressed and willingly pursued. This chapter explores the deep meaning of guidance from wise people, drawing from the Scriptures and stories of people who have sought counsel and gained insightful understanding. It also offers helpful advice on how to ask and receive counsel from others.

The Bible is filled with examples of how important seeking advice from others was in the lives of God's people. One such example is the biblical story of Moses, which is found in Exodus 18. Moses, being wise, went to his father-in-law, Jethro, for advice, and Jethro's advice not only made Moses's load lighter but also helped the Israelites become more organized.

This biblical story demonstrates the life-changing power of seeking advice from others, as demonstrated by Proverbs 11:14 (ESV): "Where there is no guidance, a people falls, but in an abundance of counselors, there is safety."

There is a plethora of examples in modern life of people seeking counsel and benefiting from sound recommendations. Some examples include young entrepreneurs who sought the counsel of seasoned mentors, married couples who sought counseling to work through difficulties, and individuals who were struggling with a significant career decision and sought advice from career coaches. These experiences highlight the practical value of seeking counsel from individuals with insightful knowledge.

Proverbs 12:15 (ESV) states, "The way of a fool is right in his own eyes, but a wise man listens to advice." It is essential to identify areas that require guidance, approach potential sources of wisdom with humility and openness, and create a nurturing environment where the counselor and the person seeking counsel can engage in a constructive dialogue.

Proverbs 19:20 (ESV) suggests we should "listen to advice and accept instruction, that you may gain wisdom in the future." This chapter also highlights the significance of distinguishing between well-meaning advice and guidance that is consistent with your values and convictions. Seeking counsel is about more than unquestioningly adhering to every piece of advice. Instead, it is about selecting the wisdom that is consistent with your understanding and convictions and grounded in the Word of God.

This is an invaluable lesson: by embracing the practice of seeking counsel, we not only benefit from the wisdom of others but also foster deeper connections and shared wisdom in our faith journey. Seeking counsel from others, grounded in biblical wisdom, can provide clarity, perspective, and a path forward in seeing our prayer come to pass.

CHAPTER 8: PRAY FOR HEALTHY RELATIONSHIPS

This chapter examines the significance of seeking divine insight in matters of love and relationships, drawing inspiration from the Scriptures; it offers helpful advice on incorporating prayer into dating, marriage, and family dynamics; it addresses the role of seeking counsel from seasoned couples or relationship experts; and it examines biblical principles for fostering and maintaining healthy relationships. The intricate fabric of our relationships makes the importance of seeking God's guidance and wisdom evident.

As stated in Proverbs 3:5–6 (ESV): "Trust in the Lord with all your heart, and do not lean on your understanding," seeking God's counsel is crucial when it comes to concerns of the heart. When we make prayer an essential part of dating, courting, and marriage, we invite divine wisdom to direct our decisions and actions. "In all your ways, acknowledge him, and he will make straight your paths." Prayer is a transformative tool for building healthy relationships. It involves seeking God's wisdom and guidance throughout the various stages of love and partnership.

The Bible is full of principles for fostering and maintaining healthy relationships. Ephesians 4:2-3 (ESV) reminds us of humility, gentleness, patience, and love in our interactions. 1 Corinthians 13:4-7 (ESV) eloquently describes the attributes of love, encouraging us to embody kindness, selflessness, and forgiveness. In addition, seeking counsel from experienced couples or relationship experts can provide valuable insights into maintaining healthy relationships. Proverbs 15:22 (ESV) advises, "Without counsel, plans fail, but with many advisers, they succeed." Wise counsel can help couples navigate challenges, understand one another better, and strengthen the foundations of their relationship.

To create strong, long-lasting, and God-centered relationships, we may embrace these values via prayer for healthy relationships, which entails asking God for direction and making a commitment to carry out these principles in our everyday interactions with our loved ones.

Through prayer and applying biblical principles that foster and maintain healthy relationships, we can nurture love and connection that glorifies God and enriches our lives. This chapter serves as an invitation to investigate the beneficial power of prayer in the area of relationships and to incorporate divine wisdom into dating, marriage, and family dynamics.

CHAPTER 9: PRAYER AND FINANCIAL STEWARDSHIP

This chapter examines the place of prayer in everyday financial matters, drawing inspiration from the Scriptures. It delves into aligning financial decisions with biblical teachings on stewardship and generosity, offers helpful advice for managing finances by God's principles, and emphasizes the significance of consulting financial advisors or experts when making financial decisions. As it relates to the challenges of our financial lives, the role of prayer in seeking financial wisdom and provision is profoundly significant.

An excellent place to start is Proverbs 3:9–10 (ESV), which emphasizes the biblical concept of stewardship and the relationship between our financial choices and God's blessings. It says, "Honor the Lord with your wealth and with the first fruits of all your produce; then your barns will be filled with plenty, and your vats will be bursting with wine."

By integrating prayer into our financial decisions and pursuits, we ask divine direction to guide our paths and decisions. Prayer plays a transforming role in our financial stewardship. It entails requesting God's wisdom and provision for our financial needs.

Living out values like tithing, helping those in need, managing resources sensibly, and avoiding the traps of debt are all part of aligning our financial decisions with biblical teachings on stewardship and generosity. 2 Corinthians 9:7 (ESV) emphasizes the significance of purposeful and joyful giving: "Each one must give as he has decided in his heart, not reluctantly or under compulsion, for God loves a cheerful giver."

A person seeking God's guidance through prayer should also seek advice from financial advisors or experts. Proverbs 11:14 (ESV) states, "Where there is no guidance, the people fall, but in an abundance of counselors there is safety."

Wise counsel can offer valuable insights into managing investments, planning for the future, and making financial decisions that align with biblical principles. Practical advice for managing finances according to God's principles includes budgeting, living within one's means, avoiding debt, and being generous in giving. These practices reflect the biblical principles of stewardship and financial responsibility.

Seeking God's guidance and financial counsel, we can manage our finances in a way that honors He ensures economic well-being. This chapter serves as an invitation to investigate the transformative power of prayer in the area of financial stewardship, to integrate divine wisdom into economic decisions, and to draw inspiration from biblical principles of generosity and wise stewardship.

CHAPTER 10: SEEK GODLY WISDOM AND DISCERNMENT

This chapter explores the significance of wisdom and discernment, drawing inspiration from the Scriptures; it explores how to apply prayer in seeking divine wisdom for making wise decisions; it explores biblical passages and narratives that underscore the value of godly wisdom; and it emphasizes the importance of seeking counsel from wise and spiritually mature individuals when faced with significant life decisions. Wisdom and discernment play an indispensable role in the complex constructs of daily life.

Prayer is an invaluable instrument in seeking divine wisdom and discernment. It involves opening our hearts to God's guidance and seeking His wisdom for our choices. By making prayer an integral part of our decision-making process, we invite divine insight to illuminate our path. Proverbs 2:6 (ESV) reminds us, "For the Lord gives wisdom; from his mouth come knowledge and understanding." This verse underscores the divine source of wisdom and its pivotal role in making sound choices.

The book of Proverbs, in particular, offers a wealth of wisdom and valuable insights. Proverbs 3:13–14 (ESV) states, "Blessed is the one who finds wisdom, and the one who gets understanding, for the gain from her is better than gain from silver and her profit better than gold." The Bible contains passages and narratives highlighting the value of godly wisdom.

Furthermore, the stories of people like Solomon, who prayed to God and was granted abundant knowledge demonstrate the transformational potential of divine wisdom. These stories encourage us to pray for wisdom because it is a priceless tool for overcoming life's challenges.

Proverbs 15:22 (ESV) states, "Without counsel, plans fail, but with many advisers, they succeed." Seeking counsel from wise and spiritually mature individuals can offer insightful advice when making important life decisions. This is why seeking counsel from wise and mature individuals, in addition to prayer, is so important.

By incorporating these principles into our lives, we can confidently navigate life's complexities and make wise, God-honoring decisions. This chapter serves as an invitation to investigate the transformative power of prayer in seeking divine wisdom and discernment. It also serves as an inspiration to draw from the biblical value of godly wisdom and to recognize the importance of seeking counsel from wise and spiritually mature individuals.

CHAPTER 11: USING PRAYER TO SPARK A KINGDOM IMPACT

The miraculous power of prayer and how it inspires us to engage in acts of service, advocacy, and mission are explored in this chapter, which draws inspiration from the Scriptures to show how prayerful Action has historically made a significant impact. The Scriptures remind us of the life-changing effect of prayer. As James 5:16 (ESV) states, "The prayer of a righteous person has great power as it is working." Prayer is how we tap into this extraordinary source of strength and guidance.

Prompted by divine guidance, prayer is not only a passive act but a dynamic force that drives us to engage in acts of service, advocacy, and mission. This call to Action is encapsulated in Isaiah 6:8 (ESV). "And I heard the voice of the Lord saying, 'Whom shall I send, and who will go for us? Then I said, "Look at me! Please send me."
The prophet Elijah's prayer for rain in 1 Kings 18:41–45 (ESV) ended a severe drought and showed how prayerful action can change the course of nature. Similarly, the book of Acts recounts that the apostle Paul's missionary journeys were marked by fervent prayer and impactful ministry. These biblical figures offer us vivid examples of prayerful action that significantly impacted us.

Praying as a catalyst for kingdom impact means figuring out where our advocacy, mission, or service can have a positive effect. Prayer gives us the courage to act with compassion and purpose, whether through mission work, social justice advocacy, or volunteering at a local shelter.

Inspired by the biblical examples of individuals who had a lasting influence through prayerful action, this chapter offers an invitation to embrace the incredible power of prayer and its function as a catalyst for kingdom impact. By living a life embedded in prayer and action, we can become instruments of change for the good of our world and, more so, for the glory of God.

SUMMARY

Congratulations, dear reader, on finishing this life-changing journey of prayer, faith, and Action! We have covered a lot in these pages, including the depths of prayer and the significance of seeking God's wisdom, discernment, and guidance in our lives; we have also looked at the art of active waiting, the dynamic relationship between faith and Action, conquering seemingly insurmountable challenges, and the priceless practice of seeking advice from knowledgeable mentors and other believers. But remember that knowledge without Action is like a seed dormant in the ground, waiting for the right opportunity to sprout into life.

Now that you've finished reading this book, it's time to put these realizations into practice, these ideas into transformation, and these words into deeds. You've discovered that prayer is more than just a ritual; it's a sacred dialogue with the One who loves you without conditions. Don't let your prayers stay just words; put them into Action. Seek God's direction in all of your decisions, big and small. Actively wait with patience and trust, knowing that His timing is perfect.

It's time to take bold steps, step out in faith, and let your actions be a testament to your unwavering trust in the One who guides your every move. You will encounter challenges along the way, but don't give up; with faith and perseverance, mountains can be moved. Seek advice from those who have gone before you, for their wisdom can be a compass during life's storms. Whether it's raising a family, managing your finances, or making important decisions in life, you must seek God's wisdom and surround yourself with a community of believers.

Now is the time to put what you've learned into practice. Take a step, decide, reach out to someone in need, and let your life be a living example of the power of faith in Action—a beacon of hope in a world that sorely needs it. As you close this book, I challenge you to let it become a well-worn companion on your faith journey. May the lessons learned within these pages be a constant reminder that you are not alone and are equipped with the tools of prayer, guidance, wisdom, and the support of fellow believers.

Your actions today can shape a brighter tomorrow for yourself and those whose lives you touch. The time for Action is now. May your journey be purposeful, guided by prayer, and empowered by the God who listens and responds to the faithful. Go and make a difference in the world with unwavering hope and determination. Remember, you are not just a reader of this book but also a participant in the ongoing story of God's work in the world.

Please write a review on Amazon.com if this book has been a blessing to you so that others can also benefit from it.

Thank you for taking this journey with me through 'What do you do after you have prayed?" If these words have resonated with you, I invite you to explore more of my writingsof inspiring books on Amazon that delve into spirituality, personal growth, and the human experience. Books include: Saved but Struggling, Well but Wounded: The Benefits of Professional Christian Counseling; Be Made Whole: The 5 Dimensions of Healing; and 10 Obstacles to Your Healing. Your ongoing support means the world to me.